# Sean Scully
# Paintings

Catalogue published for the exhibition

# Sean Scully
# Paintings

Manchester City Art Galleries
7 June - 13 July 1997

Exhibition organised by Manchester City Art Galleries
Exhibition curated by Tim Wilcox
Exhibition Programme co-ordinator: Howard Smith

Catalogue designed by Chrissie Morgan

Printed by The Pale Green Press, London

ISBN 0 901673 54 4

Catalogue essays and text ©Manchester City Art Galleries and the authors 1997

Cover photograph © Hans Namuth
Back cover:  London Studio, October 1995

**Manchester**
making it happen

NATIONAL HERITAGE · ARTS SPONSORSHIP SCHEME

Exhibition sponsored by
WILLIS CORROON FINE ART

Willis Corroon Fine Art is an award winner under the Pairing Scheme
(the National Heritage Arts Sponsorship Scheme) for its support of
Manchester City Art Galleries' Sean Scully Paintings exhibition.
The Pairing Scheme is a Government Scheme managed by ABSA
(Association for Business Sponsorship of the Arts).

# sean scully

# Paintings

Sean Scully in his London Studio 1994
Photo: Catherine Lee

# Foreword & Acknowledgements

Sean Scully enjoys a world-wide reputation as one of the foremost abstract painters working today. His paintings are apparently created from the simplest of formal means yet they are imbued with emotional effect. They are both beautiful and commanding, their surfaces rich with nuances of colour and texture . This select retrospective of Sean Scully's work from the last decade is the artist's first exhibition of paintings in a public gallery in this country since his retrospective at the Whitechapel Gallery, London in 1989. It coincides with the retrospective of the artist's drawings, *Sean Scully/Works on Paper* organised by the Staatlich Graphische Sammlung in Munich and shown at the Whitworth Art Gallery, Manchester. This provides a rare opportunity to see a significant body of his work in depth.

Our thanks are due first and foremost to Sean Scully, with whom we have worked closely on the selection of works and on all other aspects of the exhibition. He has been exceptionally generous with his time. We have also benefitted greatly from the ceaseless efforts of Sean Scully's assistant Per Haubro Jensen in New York and Tim Taylor in London has also kindly offered his help. Mark Glazebrook has contributed a thoughtful insight into the development of Scully's work and we are also fortunate to be able to have a new interview with the artist by Irving Sandler. Without the kind support of the lenders this exhibition would not have been possible and I would like to extend to them my thanks for so generously agreeing to part with their pictures for the duration of the show.

We have been fortunate in securing the generous support of Willis Corroon Fine Art and I would like to thank Louise Hallett for the work she has done on our behalf. This marks the first of three exhibitions they have agreed to support and we are extremely grateful for their assistance. This sponsorship has been matched by an award under the ABSA Pairing Scheme and our thanks are due to Chris Pulleine of ABSA North for his support. Alistair Smith of the Whitworth Art Gallery collaborated closely to allow us to combine our publicity and I would like to thank both him and his staff. I would also like to thank Tony Scully for his assistance and George Pinder of the City Treasurer's Insurance Department for his advice. Finally I would like to thank the City Art Galleries' own staff, in particular Howard Smith, Tim Wilcox, Kate Farmery and Chrissie Morgan who have worked on this project and brought it to fruition.

**Richard Gray**
**Director of Galleries and Museums**

# Sean Scully:
# Summarising Living and Painting

## Mark Glazebrook

The paintings of Sean Scully's mature period since 1981 seem to hover and vibrate with bridled emotion on a knife-edge between the Apollonian and the Dionysan. A sense of beauty and a passionate force join in an uniquely surprising asymmetric balance. An austere respect for order contains a lyric poet's feeling of both joy and melancholy. Classical in origin, a sense of discipline and harmony appears to be restraining a naturally romantic soul from expressionistic excess - but not from expression. A painterly and expressive way of animating the surface is constrained by an almost linear and geometrical approach to composition. Movement and equilibrium combine with a whole range of dualities and contrasts including warm and cool colour, dramatically and subtly dark and light tone, to create an exhilarating whole. It is as though a variety of concerns that have long occupied artists of different and opposed tendencies are compressed and resolved in Scully's recent painting.

Directness and finesse, simplicity and complexity also co-exist in Scully's work, which communicates in various connected ways. Going above the level of its status as a growing body of handsome physical objects which relate to life in the visible world in various ways, and going beyond the intellectual level of the stance it takes towards art history, there is a plateau with a bracing but rarefied atmosphere where mundane values are ultimately transcended. Here many elements and influences are condensed, distilled, married and *summarised*, as it were, in the service of Scully's high and humanistic ambitions for abstraction.

Artist's statements, notoriously prone to misconstruction, at the very least show how a particular mind is working at a given moment. Scully has put his aspirations into words, thereby recording the challenges he has set himself and offering both an insight and a focus for discussion and criticism. During the 1970s for example when still living in England Scully put forward a startling ambition; to synthesise Pollock and Mondrian. It is not so unusual to empathise with the very different spirits of these two pioneering giants in an age when the internal magic of culture after culture is available in diluted form for general study and enjoyment; but the notion of such a synthesis could only have occurred to an artist of an extremely dialectical disposition. In practice of course not everything was deemed capable of synthesis; the main elements selected were to do with composition, the non-relational all-over

6

approach of the American and the ordered relational approach of the European. From 1975 onwards, when Scully started living in New York he came more and more to think of Rothko as the Abstract Expressionist who meant most to him. The evidence of Scully's seriousness about a synthesis however, a sort of trans-national dualism, is still there in his paintings, attracting attention on both sides of the Atlantic, and even the Pacific.

In 1991, taking it for granted as he does that the purpose of art is to represent human nature, Scully expressed his desire to go beyond showing "a fragment of human nature as intensely as possible" which he saw as the traditional domain of Abstract Art. Instead his task was "to find a way to show as much of human nature as possible: *through abstraction*".[1] The charge of inhumanity had long been levelled against non-objective art. Here was a head-on counter attack. In 1993, less controversially, he appeared to express a modern equivalent of Matisse's famous dream of "an art of balance, of purity and serenity" to soothe "every mental worker........... like a good armchair in which to rest after physical fatigue". Scully wrote; "To paint as I do requires faith and implies a belief in human nature and our future. So at its best it is positive. I want people to be able to take a feeling from my work, that they can use in their lives and is sustaining".[2]

ill.1
Tonio 1984

The capacity of an art object to embody spiritual and human values and feelings, and to communicate a transcendental aura is of course deeply mysterious and complex. Whether or not there is an inclination for analysis or for an attempt to look harder or go higher or deeper, what can hardly fail to strike any viewer about Scully's oil paintings is their sheer physical presence. The strong tangible aspect of their identity is enhanced by their tendency to be multi-sectioned. The size alone, circa eight foot by twelve foot - by no means a maximum - of paintings such as *White Window* 1988 (plate 7) is impressive. In *Cross* 1986 (plate 4) the top section overlaps the bottom. The title cannot merely refer to a geometrical arrangement. (Its predominant colours, red and black, capable of signalling blood and death combined with a central T-shape suggest the crucifixion). It may be thought of therefore as a descendant of the diptych, an altar-piece that was made to be handled as well as revered. In fact many of Scully's paintings are triptychs with three word titles. He is drawn to this format partly because of its historic connotations of pathos. *West of West* 1995 (plate 18) is a daring, stunning triptych measuring no less than nine foot by fifteen foot; orange / yellow and purple chequerboard pattern to the left, black and white horizontal bands in the centre, red with vertical blackish lines on the right. *Tonio* 1984 (ill.1) has the feel of a big collage in low relief. It is composed of four distinct but joined paintings. The parts occupy more than one plane and project a few centimetres over the edge of what would otherwise be a perfect rectangle. (Scully once said that he cut and

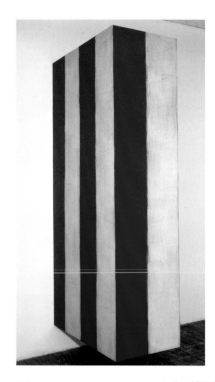

ill.2
*Floating Painting, Red White*
*1995*

edited his material like a film director).  Amongst other functions, these devices confirm each painting's solidity, its physical reality.  The same is partly true of what Scully calls windows, echoes of representational painting - Matisse in Tangier and Nice for example.  These small rectangles inside which the typical stripe motif is scaled down, are separate paintings literally inserted into the big work where they attract the eye at first glance, and function dynamically like a play within a play.  They set up yet another dualism, a relationship between something small and intense and something large and protective.  Unlike real, transparent windows however they operate in the space between picture plane and viewer.  As well as a contrast in scale these inserts confer a strange sense of time; some of them have been painted months or years previously.  They are windows into the recent or distant past.

Recently in the mid nineteen-nineties Scully has extended his territory into the third dimension by making a series of works which could be described as boxes; made of metal they are cantilevered out from the wall offering the spectator three distinct but joined painted surfaces, - a front and two sides, as in *Floating Painting, Red White* 1995 (ill.2).  In contrast, Frank Stella's deliberately raucous three-dimensional constructions for example are almost impossible to relate to the restrained Minimal paintings with which he made his name.  It would be a mistake to think that the distinctive identity and presence of Scully's work is tied to large scale or volume.  He does small oils on canvas or wood or board such as *Tabarca* 1994 (plate 15) and no artist is more sensitive to the intrinsic possibilities inherent in paper, in different media and in small scale.  His almost unerring, spontaneous and luminous watercolours, his hazy pastels, his gouaches, drawings, etchings and woodcuts are quite simply exquisite.  They provide further proof of the infinite variety of expression which can be wrung with feeling and discipline from what seems to be and has often been described as a limited repertoire of motifs.

Limited in one sense they obviously are but collectively they are both distinctive and memorable and it is arguable that they are less limited than might at first appear.  Scully's pervasive compositional elements are, of course, verticals, horizontals, (with the occasional diagonal), chequer-board squares and rectangles and above all the bands or strips of colour usually referred to as stripes. The very blandness of such a format is precisely what opens up such unlimited potentialities.   Scully has cited "the example of Chardin and Morandi as being two humanistic transcendental painters: it is striking to see how ordinary or banal their imagery is.  I wouldn't call it their subject matter, because that is the emotion generated in their work, which is launched from such a humble base: old jars and apples."[3]  In addition a stripe may be thought of as having a primal function in the *practice* of painting.  It can empty a brush loaded with paint in a very simple way. Faced with an empty rectangle, what could be more natural and logical than to place a stripe parallel to one edge. Another stripe now seems called for and so it goes on, offering an inexhaustible series of optical and emotional possibilities. For Scully himself the stripe was "a signifier for Modernism"[4] and therefore attractive as a "wreck of other forms of painting that had become untenable".[5] He considered that formalism was dead but he wanted to take something that had failed, "had the beauty of failure,"[6] and re-use it. It may also be argued that the stripe also has a metaphorical

ill.3
Bridge, Ireland
Photo: Bernd Klüser

relationship to the world we live in. Vertical stripes roughly sum up columns - of a newspaper or of the Parthenon - verticals and horizontals, Stonehenge. A grid composes the New York street plan; street contain zebra-crossings, nature contains zebras; warships are dazzle-camouflaged by stripes. In Ireland road signs on bridges have black and yellow chequer-board patterns and stripes (ill.3). Decorative uses of the stripe in clothes and buildings are legion. If abstraction means taking something out then to abstract the stripe with all its metaphorical, practical and decorative functions is to abstract something basic, crucial or at least familiar from the actual world as well as from the world of Abstract painting. Scully was not prepared to banish the stripe from his own work but he was determined to introduce a new and larger context for it. "At a certain point the way forward was no longer simply formal. Since formalism was dead in relation to abstraction in about 1980, I understood that the form had to be knocked down, taken apart. And not simply put together: *but put back together for a different reason*. The issue was now content, and relationships. Thus the issue of how things were painted in relation to each other became crucial. An art of relationships."[7]

Sean Scully's awareness of the world outside the studio is vivid, raising the obvious questions of its precise relationship to his art. Like Delacroix, Matisse and Paul Klee before him, in 1969 Scully visited Morocco. His imagination was greatly stimulated by seeing countless strips of stretched, dyed wool, used in the making of rugs, which hung on wooden bars in the sun to dry. *Wrapped Piece (Harvard)* 1973 (ill.4) shows some of the reverberations four years later. Colourfully banded canvas tents made abstract compositions against the sand provoking him to observe "I thought it was the most beautiful thing I had ever seen in my life".[8] A show of the work Jesus-Raphael Soto in Paris on the way home and the knowledge of stripe painting

ill.4
*Wrapped Piece (Harvard)*
1973
Carpenter Centre, Harvard
University, Cambridge,
Massachusetts

being done in both London and New York confirmed his ardour in what has been called a love affair with the stripe. The grid was much used by artists including Scully at that time but later he talked of the "sort of urban romance in the makeshifts people use to keep a place like Manhattan together, though of course that is the point - it doesn't exactly hold together. It's not contained. There's the grid of streets and the gridded buildings and then all the

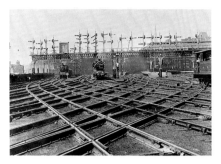

amazing things people do inside those grids and along their edges".[9] Are some of Scully's paintings since 1975 therefore a metaphor for Manhattan, like Mondrian's *Broadway Boogie-Woogie*? Armin Zweite has encapsulated the truth of the matter, with admirable caution though not in answer to this precise question, as follows: "The connection between the everyday world and the aesthetic sphere is only potential, a vague hovering suggestion which it is impossible to pin down in concrete terms - but one nevertheless senses that it is there"[10]. The photographs that Scully has taken are instructive; the crossings and

ill.5
Bridge, Newcastle-upon-Tyne

ill.6
Railway crossing, Central Station, Newcastle-upon-Tyne

ill.7
House, Mexico
Photo: Sean Scully 1987

ill.8
Stone wall, Ireland
Photo: Verena Klüser

complexities of the Newcastle-upon-Tyne railway system (ill.5 & 6) for example have conceptual similarities with his early work. His photographs of Mexican shanty town buildings(ill.7) and of the walls of Inis Meáin (ill.8) in the Aran Islands off the West Coast of Ireland have something in common. They are a mixture of vertical and horizontal elements and they record how men in an extreme situation involving survival made aesthetic as well as practical choices. They document the work of kindred spirits.

Connoisseurship and the art of attribution took a leap forward when Max Friedlander and others concentrated on the inimitability of an artist's brushwork, his personal handwriting. Scully's painting, unlike that of Bridget Riley for example (whose pictures since the 1960s have actually been painted, under supervision, by somebody else) is undelegatable. There is a clear underlying structural concept, a relic of the grid, sometimes conveying an almost bleak austerity, but the processes of layering paint, painting wet on wet, letting mysterious suppressed linear accents of colour press through at the edges between rectangles - even a deliberately rough and unfinished effect gives Scully's work a sensual, haptic aspect, which is more or less inimitable. His attitude to colour, often described as sonorous, reminding us that his favourite musical instrument is the cello, is the opposite of theoretical. He possesses a gift which has been enhanced by looking at painting, actually painting and looking at the world, memorising sensations given by walking the streets at night or observing the effect of sunrise or sunset on Mexican monuments.

His blacks are not unmitigatedly black; his whites are infinitely variable, smoky, smudgy tinged with a range of pigments. His reds resound deeply and his blurring of contours has reminded one writer[11] of Titian. Compared to his work of the early seventies in which the eye is bombarded with bright contrasts (e.g. *Red Light* 1971 ill.9) his colour since the 1980s gives an overall feeling of richness and majestic restraint. He tries to create colours on the edge of becoming another colour. Although aware of colour theory, his sense of hue and tint and tone remains subjective - regarding yellow for example which he greatly favours as "the colour of madness, jealousy and sex".[12] He reacts to sad moments in his life with dark sombre, melancholic colour. An abstractionist also paints autobiographically. Scully finds a way to paint human nature by being himself, reflecting clearly or obscurely, events and realities in his personal history, moods, strengths, risks and vulnerabilities.

ill.9
*Red Light 1971*

Scully's absorption of art history, his progress backwards and forwards through it, looking and painting, painting and looking is intriguing. Artists may be distinguished from historians by the intensity of their insight and by their partiality which is based on the cannibalistic intentions which give their love its edge: Scully is no exception. As a boy, torn from a convent school in Islington where he was happy, and thrust into a South London state school (his parents had quarrelled with the Roman Catholic Church because of their need to work seven days a week), Scully saw on the wall a fine reproduction, the sort that showed even the grain on the canvas, portraying Picasso's Blue Period painting *Child with Dove* 1901. It gave him intimations of art's power of solace. Although no serious twentieth century painter can ignore Picasso's influence or example, and he has recently talked of Picasso's "dominance" and "masculinity", Scully's passion for colour and need for transcendence was to lead him more in the direction of Matisse. Before Matisse he gravitated towards Mondrian; both artists had been forced to come to terms with both Picasso and Cubism without joining up.

In 1964 when the young Scully saw *Van Gogh's Chair* 1888 (ill.10). "It was as if the world had just stopped"[13]. The poignancy of the empty chair, the emotion conveyed by paint overwhelmed him. Something of Van Gogh's expressive directness, even some compositional elements are evident in Scully's work to this day. It is sometimes forgotten that the young Van Gogh (as well as briefly working as an art dealer) was a preacher; art came to be a sort of religion for him as it did for Scully. From Van Gogh to Fauvism is a logical step and at Croydon College, which he attended from 1965-68, Scully remembers doing big brightly coloured figurative paintings under Fauvist influence, describing himself as "crazy about" Derain - his paintings of the Thames, his complex colour, his expressionistic approach. He

ill.10
Vincent Van Gogh
*Van Gogh's Chair* 1888
©The Trustees of the
National Gallery, London

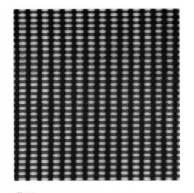

ill.11
*Soft Ending* 1969

also came to like the work of Karl Schmidt-Rotluff, Emil Nolde and Oskar Kokoschka's early period - for example *The Tempest (Windsbraut)* 1914.

The next *coup de foudre* was in 1967.  He saw the catalogue of a Rothko exhibition held at the Museum of Modern Art, New York in 1961 (he was too young to see and respond to the Whitechapel Art Gallery's counterpart later in the same year).  From that moment on he never again felt the need to make representational images.  He made a group of paintings in homage to Rothko.  Naturally his main interest then shifted to the work of abstract painters whose work he could see at first hand, such as Victor Vasarely, Mark Tobey, Gene Davis and François Morellet.  In 1969 he attempted a homage to and an intensification of Mondrian with *Newcastle Boogie-Woogie* a painting which no longer exists but *Soft Ending* 1969 (ill.11) remains a remarkable early grid painting.  *Art of the Real*, a show at the Tate Gallery, 1969 of recent American Abstraction including Minimalism had a positive effect on him.  He took the grid favoured in the nineteen-sixties by Minimal artists and others and put his own spin on it, piling grid on grid to give heightened movement and light so that they become known as supergrids - e.g. *Red Light* 1971.  In these lively paintings of the early seventies he did not imitate the work of any single artist.  He wanted above all to do something extreme in painting.  In this case it led to deliberate overcrowding.  He was concerned with dark and bright colour, shallow space, movement, rhythm, repetition, ambiguity, illusion, contrast, optical sensations, pattern, layering, translucency, opacity and light and the reconciliation of the hard-edge with the painterly.  He experimented with taping and spraying.  Such curves as appeared proved to be an endangered geometrical species.  He explored the diagonal which lead to arrow shaped paintings facing down such as *Arrival* 1973 (ill.12).  Of this painting William Feaver[14] presciently wrote that it was "like all Scully's best work, both a summary of his past preoccupations and a fresh departure".  By 1974 the diagonal all but vanished for a time and in *Overlay No.I* 1974 (ill.13) the concept of the grid all but disappeared too.  A quieter mood and tempo was signalled.  By 1974 the work of Kenneth Noland and later that of Morris Louis was of interest to Scully.  Older than himself but younger than Rothko, they were both stripe painters and interested in colour.  A problem he faced when studying and teaching at Newcastle University was that the prevailing atmosphere was not pro-Abstraction or even pro-painting in any deep emotional sense.  Pop Art was considered worthy of study and practice and the legacy of Richard Hamilton's discipleship of Marcel Duchamp lingered on.  To this day Scully regards Duchamp as "a spoiler............ who spawned mediocrity".[15]  In his head therefore, Scully was already half in New York, the capital of Abstraction where debate at the highest level between three generations of artists and critics took place.

Although New York is celebrated as the epitome of extroversion, paradoxically for Scully it was also the place where he made a great inward journey into his own soul.  Maurice Poirier begins the second chapter of his biography of

Scully as follows "Little did Scully know upon arriving in New York, in July 1975, that the next five years would take him down a path of abnegation and solitary retreat such as few artists have travelled. His quest for an art that would compete on equal terms with the most advanced formalist abstraction was to lead him virtually underground, as if into a tunnel whose exit he could reach only by purging his work of nearly all but the most fundamental elements. As earnestly as the earlier paintings had dealt with optical movement, vivid colour contrasts, and the high-spirited vitality of urban life, the new works would deal with meditative qualities and the stringencies of a Zen-like ethos. It was to be a period of intense self-purification, as well as an all-out attempt to come to grips with the very essence of artistic creation." One of the artist's Scully met in New York was Robert Ryman. He was able to view the older artist's work "quite experientially - almost out of the umbrella of art history".[16] Other influences were Agnes Martin's quiet linear approach, Brice Marden's reductivism of the 1960s, Frank Stella's and Ad Reinhardt's paintings of the 1950s.

The gradual way in which Scully emerged from his chrysalis between 1979 and 1981 is fascinating. Rather like Mondrian's development of Abstraction from paintings of trees, each work of Scully's incorporated something from a previous work and took it a step further. His gift for summarising and moving on already noted by William Feaver was now free of the frenzy of the early seventies. By 1982 the ordered evolutionary break away from Minimalism which signals

Scully's main contribution to the unfolding of art history became rapid. In the mid-seventies he had produced intensifications of the grid patterns favoured by the Minimalists. Now it was as if he turned back from the looming *cul-de-sac* long predicted for Abstraction and began to revitalise and enrich the abstract tradition by looking at a far greater length and breadth of art history than most Minimalists thought worthwhile. Art history was by no means the only ingredient in his work. When Scully executed *Heart of Darkness* 1982 (ill.14, p.14), he was thinking of Joseph Conrad's novel and the savage primal beauty of the African jungle. He also poured into it the terrible pain he felt following his own son's tragic death in a car accident. *Heart of Darkness* was a breakthrough painting in many respects. He began to rediscover the expressive possibilities in the substance of paint. He broke through to a structure which would monitor without suppressing the powerful feelings he wished to convey. *Passenger, White, White* 1995 (plate 19) with its gently modulated whites and pale blues is at the opposite end of the scale to *Heart of Darkness* in feeling - full of light and with an air of transcendence. It is worth noting that *West of West* 1995 (plate 18), a large triptych which has a completely different mood, an extraordinarily daring and precarious balance of playful contrasts, shares certain basic characteristics with *Heart of Darkness.*

ill.12
*Arrival* 1973
National Gallery of Victoria
Felton Bequest, Melbourne

ill.13
*Overlay No.1* 1974
Photo: John Webb

ill.14
*Heart of Darkness* 1982
Art Institute of Chicago,
Illinois

Conrad is among a group of novelists and poets that Scully admires, and which includes Nabokov, Becket and Joyce. All are *emigrés* like himself - and Mark Rothko. He greatly admires the ability to master and add to the language of another culture whether it is literature, music or painting. Published writing on Scully's art often reveals as much about the writer's country of origin as it does about the artist himself. That so much has been written which is both valid and different betokens a certain universality in his work. To pin down and emphasise the precise influence of a particular Italian quattrocento painter on actual works by Scully (his favourites are Cimabue and Duccio) would be to court accusations of overstatement. So much has become internalised: but if we like Scully's paintings it may be that it is partly because we like the painters he has been influenced by. Many writers for example have sensed Scully's affinity with Velasquez in an almost palpable way. It is not just to do with the use of blacks and silvery greys, it is something to do with the capacity of paint to simulate the texture of flesh or the material of a dress - plus an aura of simple grandeur. Velasquez was thought of in the late nineteenth century as a precursor of Impressionism. R.A.M Stephenson went so far as to end his influential monograph on Velasquez by calling him "the great Spanish Impressionist". The concentration on tonal relationships or tonal painting in the Velasquez-Manet tradition, which included Whistler, was talked of and taught in art schools. Certain painters with a special feeling for tone and colour have tuned in to the magical capacity of a painting to generate its own light. It is a great tradition with has nothing to do with Conceptualism or didacticism and it connects Scully to many of the artists he is drawn to and who have inspired him. Luminosity has a further connection with the transcendental world which Christian artists of the Middle Ages and Renaissance searched for, which Mondrian sought through Theosophy and Rothko reached through meditation and contemplation, brush in hand.

It is not by accident that many of Scully's paintings include the word light in the title. *Stone Light*, 1992 (Bayerische Staatsgemäldesammlungen, Munich) (ill15), for example is regarded as one of his finest works. Scully's own brushwork is a world of its own. He uses a systematic structure to make paintings like walls - but walls that dissolve with light. An infinite variety of brushstrokes light or heavy, large or small, neat or untidy, going this direction or that, combine with inflecting hues, tones and thicknesses of paint to create opacity, translucency and light. His ability to evoke unique sensations by moving paint on the surface of canvas is at the heart of his power to communicate his understanding of the 'radiant and humanistic possibilities for painting'. He sees the structure within which he works as being imbued with the typical experiences of modern life, "its repetitions, dislocations, parallel realities, abrupt conclusions and beginnings."[17]

A Celtic soul survives geographical separation and Scully is fully aware of his Irish roots; but it is his destiny to belong nowhere - - and everywhere. England gave him an education and an introduction to foreign art. London gave him his taste for great cities, the intellectual and commercial centres to which artists and writers have often been drawn whatever their nationality. Scully refuses to be assimilated by a single culture. He wants to express the contradictions in the human spirit. At a lecture in Dublin in 1994 he quoted Schiller, Simone Weill and Nietzsche at the outset - adding his own epigrammatic observation: "We have more than one soul". Sean Scully needed to enter the older cultures of different European countries while continuing to experience the modern dynamism of America. His summarising talent, incorporating elements from his own nature, from life itself, from each stage of his own work, combined with an ability to digest deeply and bring together almost antithetical aspects of more than one tradition help to explain the vital tension in his work. It gives him the unique position that he occupies today and brings a surge of renewed faith in the future of the ancient art of painting itself.

ill. 15
*Stone Light* 1992
Bayerische
Staatsgemäldesammlungen,
Munich

**Mark Glazebrook**
**April 1997**

**Footnotes**

**1.** My italics. Artist's written statement 28 August 1991.

**2.** Artist's written statement 8 November 1993.

**3.** Conversation with the writer 14 April 1997.

**4.** Ibid.

**5.** Artist's statement, Hugh Lane Memorial Lecture, Dublin 1994.

**6.** Ibid.

**7.** Conversation with the writer 13 April 1997.

**8.** Maurice Poirier, *Sean Scully*. Hudson Hill Press, New York, 1990, p.16.

**9.** Armin Zweite 'To Humanise Abstract Painting: Reflection on Sean Scully's Stone Light. October 1973'. Translated by John Ormrod. From *Sean Scully: Twenty Years*, 1977-99 pub. by Thames & Hudson 1995 with the High Museum of Art, Atlanta, Georgia.

**10.** Ibid.

**11.** Victoria Combalia, 'Sean Scully: Against Formalism'. *From Sean Scully: Twenty Years*, 1977-99 pub. by Thames & Hudson 1995 with the High Museum of Art, Atlanta, Georgia.

**12.** From an interview with Hans-Michael Herzog, *Sean Scully: The Catherine Paintings,* Kunsthalle, Bielefeld, p.79.

**13.** Maurice Poirier, *Sean Scully*. Hudson Hill Press, New York, 1990, p.14.

**14.** Art International / The Lugano Review, November 1973, Vol. XVII/9.

**15.** Conversation with the writer 31 March 1997.

**16.** Maurice Poirier, *Sean Scully*. Hudson Hill Press, New York, 1990, p.61.

**17.** Artist's written statement 13 April 1995.

plate 1
**1.** *River* 1984


plate 2
**2.** *Stare* 1984


plate 3
**3.** *Tonio* 1984

plate 1

plate 2

plate 3

plate 4
**4.** *Cross* 1986


plate 5
**5.** *A Happy Land* 1987


plate 6
**6.** *Battered Earth* 1988

plate 4

plate 5

plate 6

plate 7
**7.** *White Window* 1988


plate 8
**8.** *Without* 1988


plate 9
**9.** *Red Painting* 1989

plate 7

plate 8

plate 9

plate 10
**10.** *Inisher* 1990


plate 11
**11.** *Skerry* 1992


plate 12
**12.** *Eriskay* 1992

plate 10

plate 11

plate 12

plate 13
**13.** *Rona* 1992

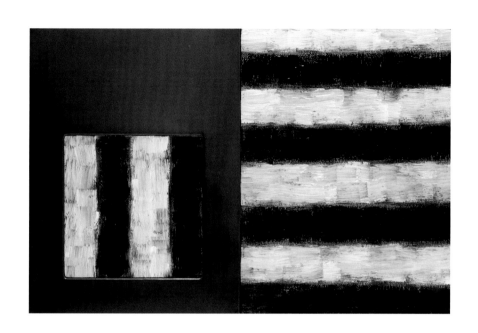

plate 14
**14.** *Coll* 1993

# Sean Scully interviewed by Irving Sandler

**Irving Sandler:** I thought that maybe we would start at the beginning with the simplest question of all. How did you become an artist? What brought you from a working class background in Ireland - you would have already moved to England.

Sean Scully: Yes.

**IS: At what age did you come to England?**

SS: When I was two I think.

**IS: So your turning to art would have happened in England?**

SS: Oh yeah.

**IS: How did that come about?**

SS: Well I think ... its very difficult of course to know how these things happen but as far as I can remember I would say that when we came to England we went into what one could describe as an immigrant ghetto situation, you know with Irish people, and I went to a convent school. My memory of that was that it was a place full of mystery and ritual that was a difficult environment but it was an extraordinarily interesting environment because it was concerned with issues that are spiritual and there was a lot of visual stuff to accompany that. You know I went to a little church that was next to the school. The school was quite humble and the church was really a shack, more or less a tin shack. Now its a community centre. And when I broke, when my parents broke with the Catholic Church, and took me out of there because there was a big fight about them working seven days a week, I went to a state school and this was a traumatic shock for me. So I was moved from a world of ideas and a world that was quite delicate, where the children were quite delicate, into a world that was grey, hard, spirituality empty and very violent - the state school in other words. I can describe it to you in colour. One was black, white and red and the one I entered was grey and it was made of stone and it was very frightening to me and I think that's when my ... my need to replace that sense of loss began and I started to get interested in being an artist. When I was in these schools, these various state schools, I generally tended to be the school artist.

**IS:     Were there teachers that encouraged you?**

SS:     Well yeah, all the teachers loved to have the ... have the little boy who was the artist. They all think its great because when you go to children's school then you have one teacher for everything and then the teacher has somebody who's going to make all the scenery in the school play and make all the puppets for the school puppet show. So that was me.

**IS:     What about later on when you actually decided to go to art school. Was there support from your family or were they opposed to it? What were the pressures for and against?**

SS:     I think that they didn't oppose it or encourage it. I think that they were unsure of what it was. Though I must say that my mother was a singer and my parents are now very good dancers.

**IS:     Were they then too?**

SS:     No. But my family, in very reduced circumstances, had artistic aspirations because I think of the Irish culture as being one that's very much concerned with knowledge and there's a great respect for books and for literature as you know.

**IS:     Sure.**

SS:     And this is very important in the culture of the Irish. So people would speak and use words in a way that was very poetic, very gentle, in relation to what I would describe as the efficiency of the English culture which you know yourself first hand since you've lived there part time. So you know what I'm talking about. The sensibility is different between an Irish sensibility and an English or London sensibility. And so there were examples for me. You couldn't describe anybody as an artist in the professional sense except my mother, she came very close to being a successful professional singer, but the people were poetic and artistic by inclination. So it is in the culture, it's in the atmosphere.

**IS:     Let's now take you into art school. Tell me about the process of even deciding that and then choosing a school and beginning to study art there.**

SS:     Well what happened to me was that I left school at the earliest opportunity.  At fifteen I worked in the print, I worked as a messenger, I worked in a graphic design studio,  I worked on building sites.  I did everything.  I had many many jobs and I was a kind of teenage adventurer. I had a discotheque that I started up and that kind of thing.

IS:     **What city was this?**

SS:     This was all in London. After we left Ireland.

IS:     **All in London?**

SS:     Yeah.

IS:     **So your family then moved to London from Ireland?**

SS:     Yeah.  We always lived in London.

IS:     **OK.  And go on with this part of your life.**

SS:     So I would say that my adolescence was not wasted on books.  It was an adventure.  It was living ... living life to the hilt and I became very infatuated with American music.

IS:     **Jazz that would be?**

SS:     No that was blues.

IS:     **Blues.**

SS:     Blues and American rock and roll and so on.  And all the attendant roots.  I became very enamoured with things American and American movies.  They represented a lot of heroism and opened up possibilities to me.  At about the age of 18 I started to look at paintings again from not looking at paintings when I was teenager, you know, because then I was more interested in other things as you can imagine.  Principally girls.

IS:     At age 18 ... what year would that have been?

SS:     That would have been in 1963 when London was starting to be the centre of the universe which it really was in the '60s. London was the most incredible place in the '60s. Maybe San Francisco could be compared with it as the two most interesting places for a kind of explosion of romantic idealism and hipness. Anyway I was really in it to the hilt and into the music scene and I started to look at paintings and something about paintings has always profoundly moved me and I think that it must have its root in this kind of poetic Irish sensibility that I grew up in. This love of beauty, this love of knowledge, this love of things other ... outside normality. And of course then there were the Stations of the Cross paintings that were in that little church ... you know they were very touching. They weren't probably any good you know, but they were paintings, and when you're a kid you don't really care so much what they're about. The fact that they're paintings is what's fascinating and that they tell stories and they make you have feelings. So that was early, that was early information. And then when I was about eighteen I started to want to go to art school desperately. So then I had to go to night school.

IS:     Before that what pictures were you looking at? Did you go to the National Gallery ....

SS:     I went to the Tate and I looked at the Post-Impressionists. I loved them ... loved them.

IS:     But at that point would there have been more contemporary art, say the new Pop Art that was emerging or ...

SS:     Yeah but I wasn't interested in that. I was interested in figurative painting. And I was interested in this world of colour that you could have: coloured, subjective realism and that to me was very exciting because its full of contradiction of course, that combination. And I started to go to the Tate in my own time. I loved these paintings, I loved the way nature could be painted, especially the work of Vincent Van Gogh and that sense of rhythm. And I've always loved rhythm. His work is very linear too of course. It doesn't really have a great sense of volume. Its flat linear so it has a kind of rhythmic quality, musical quality.

IS:     Then you went to night school.

SS:     Yeah.

IS:     Which one?

SS:     Oh I went to any night school that would help me to get educated.

IS:     **Oh in other words you were going for a degree in order to go to art school.**

SS:     Yeah.  I was trying to get my school leaving certificate.  I didn't have anything.

IS:     **Right.**

SS:     I was just a working class boy.

IS:     **Right.**

SS:     And I must say that the guys I worked with were quite wonderful because they knew that I wanted to go to art school and whenever there was time they would always let me do drawing or something.  You know on the building sites or wherever.  And they knew I was going to a night school so they would let me knock off early.

IS:     **Oh great.**

SS:     They were very sweet to me so that was wonderful.  I would go directly from work to night school and I was going to night school a lot you know and that takes a lot of discipline when you're a teenager.  Anyway I worked very hard.  I got into a remedial art school I would call it, Croydon, and I got turned down by eleven other art schools.  Every single art school in London that you can think of turned me down.  Every single one.  I used to come home and I used to sit there in a puddle of tears saying they won't give me a chance.  And I didn't know what to do.  I would run round to the next interview full of enthusiasm and leave knowing I hadn't got in again.  That they didn't like what I did.  Because basically I didn't have any talent you see.  All I had was this kind of burning will and this desire to ... to do it.  But the thing about me is, as you probably noticed over the years that we've known each other, my spirit is ... its virtually unstoppable.  Once I want to do something I have so much optimism that it takes a truck wreck to stop me.  Eventually I got into a place called Croydon which is where all the unqualified people go and that's where I went.  And then I continued my education and eventually I was very good at passing exams.  Then I had enough academic material to go to university.  I went from Croydon to Newcastle University which is a very good art school.

IS:     **That takes us to what year roughly?**

SS:     Well I guess that would be about '65 when I went to Croydon, when I was 20.

IS:     **Then when did you go to Newcastle?**

SS:     About '68. Because it took me about three years to get out ... to get out of Croydon.

IS:     **You were age 23.**

SS:     Yeah that's right. Because I graduated when I was 26.

IS:     **What was Newcastle like?**

SS:     Newcastle was really interesting and I'm incredibly happy I went there. Its a town, as you know, with beautiful bridges.

IS:     **Yes.**

SS:     Iron bridges.

IS:     **Yes.**

SS:     And they influenced the early paintings I made. Overlapping grid paintings. Because I would drive in and out of Newcastle all the time and I would drive past these bridges and they would make a big impact on me. It had a wonderful sense of space Newcastle because its a fortress town surrounded by rivers and the people there are very interesting. They are right on the edge of being English, they're almost not English any more.

IS:     **Right.**

SS:     It's the last stop before Scotland.

IS:     **Yes.**

SS:     I used to work in a gas station two nights a week. I used to sleep on the floor with an old dog - a guard dog. It was very ferocious to anybody who would try to come in and all the trucks going from London to The North would stop there. This was the Old Roman Road, this was the last stop where they could gas up. And I would sit there and write poetry while I made money pumping gasoline. I would sit there and I work these poems up. But in the end I found that poems, the poetry started to interfere too much with the painting because, you know, I found when you write poetry you have to get up in the night all the time and write ... write poems that you keep thinking of. And in the day I would be so exhausted I couldn't paint, so I gave up the poetry. And in Newcastle they had Kurt Schwitters' Merzbau reconstructed in the gallery. I'd see it every day. It had no influence on me at all. Interesting. Because it wasn't ... I think it wasn't spiritual enough for me or it wasn't ... it didn't have the right kind of spirituality. It wasn't strongly connected enough to the history of painting. The use of colour. And even though I was offered this influence every day, I would see it ten times a day, nothing happened. I find that very interesting. How one selects ones influences. A human being has a need to be influenced by certain things and finds these things to be influenced by. And then we all say ah yeah well you were influenced by that because you lived there. Its true but its also not true because if it was true, if it was simply like that, I would have been influenced by the Merzbau, but I wasn't. But if there had been a Rothko there I would've definitely been influenced every day going in and out of the art school.

**IS:     You were actually overlooking the river then?**

SS:     You could see it if you went to the top of one of the roofs in the university.

**IS:     And Scotland would have been on the other side of the river.**

SS:     Yeah it would have been north. 40 miles north. And we would drive up sometimes in the snow, when the snow was banked up on either side of the road we would drive up to Scotland at night just to have a drink and then drive back. It was great. Just to be even more out there. And the beaches were white. Fabulously beautiful beaches and so cold... not warm enough to take your clothes off. So of course they would be deserted. The sights up there are just fantastic. So it was interesting for me. I remember coming down to London to visit the art school were I subsequently taught, Chelsea, and I remember that all the paintings in there were kind of similar. They were the paintings that were very fashionable. And now of course they would be similar in another way but they would still be similar to each other. Now they're probably influenced by a kind of neo-conceptual thinking. You know a kind of intellectual respectability in relation to the problem of still making a painting. And all the paintings would have that flavour and at that time they all had another kind of flavour which was sub-New York Colourfield. But when you were up in Newcastle you really had no teachers and that was very interesting. Very interesting.

**IS:    What do you mean no teachers?**

SS:    Well there were professors there but they didn't really want to do anything.

**IS:    I see. So your primary interaction would have been with other students.**

SS:    Yeah. It was with other students. You made alliances with other students. When I first went there that school was a kind of neo-Dada school, post-Richard Hamilton - he taught there. But when I left it was an abstract painting school.

**IS:    Talk about what happens to your work in the process of those three years. The first work I saw was work that was done immediately after school. Some of it may even have been started in school. One might call it a sort of 'optical abstraction'. But how do you get from Post-Impressionism to that. First it would require a move into abstraction.**

SS:    Yes, that's exactly right. You're quite correct. What happened was that when I went to Croydon I learned to draw. I did life drawing every day and I applied myself to it with great passion. So I became a good realist. Then I started to be influenced by the German Expressionists and the Fauve painters and I made figurative paintings that were very coloured and quite abstract. Then I picked up a catalogue of Rothko at the Whitechapel and of course it didn't take that much to knock me over the line because I was already pregnant you know, I was ready to join up   And once I saw the profound spiritual possibilities of abstraction in Mondrian and Rothko in particular then I was very happy to be there and I made a lot of paintings that were influenced by these people at Croydon, but quite loosely painted. I was much more instinctive as a painter in Croydon than I was in Newcastle because naturally Newcastle was a more cerebral environment. So when I went to Newcastle I was still making these abstract paintings with big brushes and broad areas of colour and I started to tighten up my work at a certain point and I became more interested in the theory. My work, my paintings, became in fact much more conceptual, much more rigorous. I started to make piled up grids and they had an opticality to them but the real issue for me was the fact that they had a kind of endless space to them and that's something that still preoccupies me now, you know the sense of mystery, the sense of covering or layering has been very consistent all the way through my work really and I've always been attracted to artists that have that in them ... have that capacity in their work which runs through of course you know Rembrandt, Masaccio, Velasquez and so on. And by the time I left Newcastle, by the time I graduated I was making grid paintings that might be described as supergrids. That's when I came to the Carpenter Center at Harvard. My first time in the U.S.

**IS:**     **But by that time you were an abstract artist.**

SS:     Without question.

**IS:**     **What did abstraction mean to you?  Do you remember at that point?**

SS:     Well I think it meant to me the same thing that it fundamentally means to me now and that hasn't really changed.  I think that what I'm interested in is a kind of universality.  I want to make things that can move everybody.  I'm more interested in what unites us than what divides us and I think that there are obviously many variations on that, many possibilities of having aspects of both to various degrees in your personality.  But my feeling is that people who do work that is overtly topographical or political are very interested in what divides us and they're interested in pursuing an investigation into the expression of that.

**IS:**     **I find that outlook most interesting. Talk some more about it.**

SS;     So what I tried to do, I suppose, when I first made abstraction was to work it from that universality and, I mean, obviously its true because I pick Mondrian and Rothko as the two most spiritually generous of them all and Newman of course.  And I think what's happened is that I've understood that the world is a broken place and my work now takes that on.  It takes on the fact that the world is broken and still tries to make something that is universal, despite that.  Because I felt that as I move through time and as I live in the world in different places as I do, I became aware that the real situation was that it was fractured and always has a powerful urge to be fractured and people want to celebrate their separateness. My life has been so strange in that way you know.  Its a strange journey of placelessness, of being without place.  I mean people in Ireland like to say I'm Irish....

**IS:**     **They even gave you a postage stamp.**

SS:     They gave me a postage stamp.  But you know I speak like an English person and I paint with the vocabulary of an American artist.

42

**IS:**    And now you've moved to Spain.

**SS:**    And now I've got a situation in Spain. But all this, is, I think a kind of desperate attempt to pull the world together and I seem to be running around trying to do this out of all this kind of ... out of these broken bits and pieces. Putting them together.

**IS:**    Incidentally when you did a television show on BBC that was on ...

**SS:**    Matisse.

**IS:**    Matisse. How does he enter into this equation? Of course Newman and Rothko come from Matisse ...

**SS:**    Yes, oh absolutely.

**IS:**    There's a sort of a sensuality in Matisse's work that...

**SS:**    Yeah, yeah. There's a complexity ... a compositional complexity and dimensionality that corresponds I think to a profound human need. This is something that I took on in my work because when I think about time I'm not one of these people that thinks about time in five or ten year sections, I think about time in the way time has evolved over a century or two. I have a bigger idea of time and maybe this makes me a little out of time at times.

**IS:**    I thought I would introduce that dimension because there is this very rich sensual quality in your work as well as a more spiritual quality that one finds in a Rothko which hasn't got the body that your work has.

**SS:**    Yeah right. Now I love Rothko's work and he's probably my favourite artist, certainly of the 20th century. And I rank him right up there you with Cimabue and others whose work I love very much. But I have a lot of influences. You see my work is not just a question of one or two influences, its the result of many influences. And one of these influences is Matisse, but its also the whole European tradition which takes into account not only the body of the painting but the possibility for what I would call dimensionality of experience. I wanted to make something and do want to make something that is dimensional within each individual work. You see my feeling is that the reason people got sick and tired of painting is because it basically became very academic and my own personal theory about this is that all that kind of immigrant energy that had manifested itself in the New York School, and that the subsequent generation was able to feed off of, began to get more and more remote. This wonderful collision of European angst and density colliding with the American sense of freedom and honesty and frankness resulted in Abstract Expressionism which is beautiful: it has both.

**IS:     Yeah so you're thinking really on the one hand Pollock, possibly Clyfford Still and on the other hand De Kooning for example.**

SS:     Yeah. All working together. All in this kind of mix coming up with fantastic art. Undeniably great art. It became thinner and thinner you know where you had people using more and more and more devices to make their work look interesting. So the work ... the vocabulary changed.

**IS:     As it does.**

SS:     The vocabulary changed from ...

**IS:     Expressive to interesting.**

SS:     Precisely. And interesting is not as interesting as expressive. Its not as important to be perfectly frank. Its ... its secondary. It might be diverting, it might be erudite, enlightening and so on, but its not as great as the art of the Abstract Expressionist school and I think it lost a lot of its power, lost a lot of its relevance. It became more remote. It became more to do with a world of aristocratic collectors and aristocratic or elitist art magazines. I mean you get somebody like Count Panza di Biumo. One could compare him with the Medicis but he's more removed from life. What I wanted to do was make more contact with life so I started to think about this. I wanted to do something that was more akin to what Matisse did where the paintings are dimensional in terms of emotion and time, sentiment, what they're actually signifying. In other words to make again an art work that had the capacity to move and be involving ... involving and reflective of life. The way people really are because we're not like statues, we're not monolithic. We feel many things at the same time. We are dimensional. We are sexually complex, we are intellectually complex. We believe many things at the same time and we should have an art that can reflect that and yet be transporting or be moving. So you see I didn't want to give up one or the other. There's a very greedy energy at work here and that's really what I've been working with, that aspiration.

**IS:     Let me take you to the Carpenter Center because we're going to circle back to this again a little later.**

**How did that happen? You would have gotten out of Newcastle and there was a fellowship available?**

SS;      Yeah.  It happened the way most things have happened in my life and that is at the last minute basically.  I picked up the newspaper one day in Newcastle, I always got *The Sunday Times*.  I love reading the newspaper.  And there was an ad and it said five fellowships available for Harvard University, any discipline, and that's all it said.  And then it gave the address.  So I thought there must be an art school there.  I just wrote to the Art Department and it went to the Visual Art Center at the Carpenter Center, which is strange  And a wonderful thing happened which gives you an idea of how ritualistic I am in my behaviour, how animalistic I am or superstitious I am.  I do the same thing when I paint.  I do lots of things before I paint.  Nervous things.  Make loads of phone calls and so on and so on.  Reassure myself I'm not alone in the universe.  I got an interview.  I decided that when I went for the interview I would go and I would have my cappuccino in a nice little Italian place nearby, because it was right next to the American Embassy, and I would buy a newspaper and I would read it and then I would go in and get the fellowship.  So I got up in the morning, its pouring with rain, pouring with rain.  I mean London, like most cities, when it pours with rain it takes three times longer to get anywhere.  So by the time I got there I was really late.  I got out of the car, no umbrella.  I walked across the square where the American Embassy is.  I went to a coffee shop and it was closed.  I pleaded with the guy.  He opened it up and made me a cappuccino and while he was making the cappuccino I said I'll be back in a minute with the newspaper and went and bought the newspaper, came back, did it according to the script ...

**IS:      ... and then went in.**

SS:      I walked into the interview looking like I'd been deep-sea diving without a scuba diving outfit.  And they were so charmed by it because I'd told them the story, they gave me the fellowship.  Isn't that funny.

**IS:      That's wonderful. What was the Carpenter experience like?**

SS:      Well that was interesting.  I met a very interesting man there called Eduard Sechlar who's an architectural historian.  He kind of took me under his wing.  And I got a big studio there and I was left on my own more or less because they thought I was a special student.  Because on my registration form it said "S".  That's what they write when they don't know what you are.  It means special student.  And they didn't know whether I was a student or whether I should be invited to faculty meetings.  It's in the Corbusier Building where the sun comes in all the time.  So they invite me to a faculty meeting one day just to see ... you know get this out of the way.  Its very polite up there.  So I'm sitting there and the sun's streaming in and these guys were talking like that, with European accents you know, about what we're going to do for the tenth anniversary of the Carpenter Center and so on and so on. And I don't remember falling asleep but I remember waking up, lurching out of my seat and falling onto the table and then sitting up straight and I must have been asleep for half an hour in the faculty meeting and these guys were so polite they just carried on talking as if nothing had happened but after that they didn't invite me to any more faculty meetings because they realised that I was too irresponsible for that kind of thing. While I was there I made my work incredibly experimental. I came down to New York in a car ... an old car that I'd bought. We'd go round the galleries. I loved the Paula Cooper Gallery very much, it was my favourite gallery. And I remember speaking to her and showing her my slides and she was very nice to me.

IS:     **This now would have taken you into nineteen sixty ...**

SS:     No that was nineteen seventy ...

IS:     **... one, two.**

SS:     Two let's say yeah. Yeah 1972/1973, that was when I was at Harvard. And you know it was a very very good thing for me that I didn't come to New York because I couldn't handle it. I found it physically awesome. It would have been too much for me. But when I was in Boston, you know, I was really protected by all these people - all my friends in Lincoln. I was in a very lucky situation. So I worked ...

IS:     **Is there anything else you would like to talk about?**

SS:     We could talk just slightly more about the relationship between the painterliness of something, its ability to represent something like a skin and its ability to offer the possibility of being emotional, I'm very interested ... well I'm obsessed really, with this possibility in painting. Or, to put it another way, what makes painting so irreplaceable in a certain sense. You know these photographs which I have here which I like to do and which I'm going to start to show are, you can see, concerned with doors but a photograph, as interesting as a photograph can be, doesn't have the body of a painting, it doesn't have its sensuality and its this kind of miraculous relationship that's always fascinated me, always holds me, binds me to painting. And I think that its important right now especially not to be apologetic about wanting to make paintings and so many of my contemporaries are and I think that they have perhaps contrived a situation where they are able to be presented as a group but it takes a group to be of any interest. But that's not what ultimately one is aiming for. One is aiming for the point where one can have an exhibition of work or one can make a body of work that can occupy a huge space and involve people and keep people there and make them want to come back several times, or affect and change their lives in some way.

**IS:     So what you're saying is that painting offers some kind of expression that no other medium could offer and that is very important.**

SS:     Yeah and its not necessary to, for example, imitate photography in painting.  Because photography is interesting and photographic effects are interesting and, you know, I make photographs myself, I'm very interested in it.  But interesting is not important.  The question is what's important and what's moving and what is affecting and what is going to correspond with human nature in a way, that is important. And I think that there are thousands of possibilities … millions of possibilities in the world to be interesting.  In fact everything is more or less interesting.  And this word interesting has in a sense neutralised a lot of art.  And I think that painting has, in its capacity either a grand finale in front of it or a grand future.  Either way its very worthwhile being involved in it and devoting yourself to it.

**IS:     Let me ask you a last question and I've saved it for last because its personal.  Your companion of many years now, Cathy, what is her relationship to you as an artist because she's an artist herself … .  You've named eighteen pictures named after her - and I was curious as to how you might answer that or not at all.**

SS:     Well yeah … that is a series of paintings. Well that relationship has been a relationship that made a lot of things possible for both of us and we came here to New York and we really did help each other enormously.  And I feel very proud of the way we helped each other.  I think that what we made is really a result of how we work together and each person's work obviously expresses their own nature, which it should do, but it's definitely been informed by the advice and help … input of another human being.  There's never been the slightest competitiveness between us, its never even come up in all the time I've known her and all the time she's known me.  And I would say that our mutual assistance has been fundamental and if you have that kind of relationship I think it allows you to go a lot further.

**IS:     Absolutely.  I know it because I have a similar one.**

SS:     Yeah and its true, you know, when they say two heads are better than one.  Well there's a reason why they say that.  So if you can find someone you can work with and be with in that way then you've got a big advantage.

**February 1997**

plate 15
**15.** *Tabarca* 1994

plate 15

plate 16
**16.** *Skellig* 1995

plate 16

plate 17
**17.** *Block* 1995

plate 17

plate 18
**18**. *West of West 1995*

plate 18

plate 19
**19.** *Passenger, White, White 1997*

plate 19

# SEAN SCULLY:
## A Biographical Chronology

**1945**

Born in Dublin, Ireland on 30 June, the son of a barber.

**1949**

The family migrated to London, living at first near the Old Kent Road, (in recent years he has maintained a studio in the same vicinity) soon moving to a rambling Victorian house rented by Scully's grandmother on Highbury Hill, North London.  The house was full of relations and other Irish people.   His experience of being Irish was based on being part of an Irish community in London.  He attended convent schools.  The Roman Catholic Church including the incense and the rich visual aura was important to Scully until his father broke with it  (largely because of the need to work on Sundays).

**c.1953**

His mother and father bought a house in Sydenham, South London and he  attended state school - a much more hostile environment, in which he gained a reputation as a fighter who would defend his corner.  Years later he was to win a black belt in Karate.

**1960-62**

Worked as an apprentice in a commercial printing shop in London, then joined a graphic design studio.

**1962-65**

Having convinced his father that he wanted to become an artist, he attended evening classes at the Central School of Art, beginning by studying life drawing. His mother was musical and became a singer.

**1963**

Scully has described his own childhood as "enterprising".   He ran a discotheque in South London with his brother, Tony on the turntable until it was closed by the police for being too crowded and noisy.   The Scully brothers played rhythm and blues and rare imports such as Chuck Berry, Sunny Boy Williamson, B.B. King, John Lee Hooker and Muddy Waters.  He sang in a band - his brother playing the drums.  He started small businesses including an animal hospital.

**1964**

The overwhelming effect of seeing *Van Gogh's Chair* 1888 at the Tate Gallery made a lasting impression.

**1965**

Birth of his son, Paul Scully from his first marriage to Jill Mycroft.

**1965-68**

Studied at Croydon College of Art, London. One teacher, Ron Howard was helpful in explaining how pictures were actually made from Fragonard to Picasso for example. Another art master, Barry Hirst helped open his eyes to colour - Fauvism was discussed intensively.

**1967**

Obtained the catalogue of a Mark Rothko exhibition held six years earlier at the Museum of Modern Art, New York. From that moment he never felt the need to do another figurative painting again.

**1968-71**

Became a student at the University of Newcastle just after Victor Pasmore and Richard Hamilton had left. Scully was drawn to the influence of Ian Stephenson - a systematic, romantic, abstractionist interested in Pointillism whom the students liked.

**1969**

Spent part of the summer in Morocco. Seeing striped materials used in rug making and striped tents on the beach made a lasting impression. Exhibitions such as *Soto* in Paris and *Art of the Real* in London impressed him as did seeing a production of *Waiting for Godot* by Samuel Becket.

**1970**

Awarded the Stuyvesant Foundation Prize. (It was a purchase award which enabled the Foundation to sell the picture at a considerable profit later).

**1971-72**

Given his own studio and the post of assistant teacher at Newcastle University for a year. He was a prize winner in John Moore's Liverpool Exhibition 8.

**1972-73**

Became a graduate student at Carpenter Center at Harvard University, Cambridge, Mass. under a Frank Knox fellowship.

**1973**

Alec Gregory-Hood having seen Scully's prize winning painting at Liverpool gave him his first solo exhibition at his own gallery, the Rowan Gallery. He was to continue showing there for the next twenty years.

**1973-75**

Met the American artist, Catherine Lee in San José, California whom he was to marry in 1978. He was to make a painting in her honour every year. They were exhibited together as the Catherine Paintings in 1993 at the Fort Worth Museum of Modern Art, Texas. First exhibition on the West Coast of America at the Tortue Gallery, Santa Monica, California.

**1975**

Moved to the United States, settling in New York.

**1977**

First solo show in New York at the Duffy-Gibbs Gallery. Began teaching part time at Princeton University a post which lasted until 1983. During this period he met and was befriended by the critic and curator Sam Hunter. Also during this period he found a friend and patron in Charles Choset, the writer, composer and collector. Choset made a large collection of Scully's work's. After Choset's death in 1986, Scully dedicated an exhibition to his patron which opened at the Whitechapel Art Gallery, London in 1989.

**1981**

Ten year retrospective mounted at the Ikon Gallery, Birmingham which then travelled within the United Kingdom under the auspices of the Arts Council of Great Britain.

**1982**

Spent part of the summer working at Edward Albee's artist's colony in Montauk, Long Island.

**1983**

Received Guggenheim fellowship and had the first of many shows at the David McKee Gallery, New York. Became an American citizen. His son Paul was killed in a car accident.

**1984**

Artist's fellowship from the National Endowment for the Arts.

**1985**

First solo exhibition at an American Museum at the Carnegie Institute, Pittsburgh which travelled to the Museum of Fine Arts, Boston.

**1988**

First exhibition in Japan at Fuji Television Gallery, Tokyo.

**1989**

Major exhibition spanning the years 1982-88 held at the Whitechapel Art Gallery, London which travelled to Munich and Madrid. By now Scully was maintaining studios in both New York and London.

**1990**

*Sean Scully* by Maurice Poirier was published by Hudson Hill Press, New York; a fully illustrated monograph on his life and work to date.

**1992**

Lectured on his own work at Harvard University, during a retrospective exhibition at the museum. Revisited Morocco in December to make a film on Matisse for the BBC.

**1993**

First exhibition of the *Catherine* Paintings at the Modern Art Museum of Fort Worth, Texas.

**1994**

Lectured on his own work at the Hugh Lane Municipal Gallery of Modern Art, Dublin; the Hugh Lane Memorial Lecture. In January the French Post Office issued a limited edition stamp with a watercolour by Scully, marking Irish membership of the EEC. In November visited the Aran islands off the West Coast of Ireland.

**1995**

Participated in the Joseph Beuys lectures Ruskin School of Drawing and Fine Art, Oxford University. Acquired a studio in Barcelona from which to work. In the winter Scully lived and worked in Munich where he still maintains a studio. A travelling exhibition *Sean Scully: Twenty Years* organised by Ned Rifkin, of the High Museum, Atlanta, Georgia travelled to the Hirshhorn Museum and Sculpture Garden, Washington D.C.
*The Catherine Paintings* with the assistance of the British Council exhibited at: Kunsthalle, Bielefeld, Germany, Palais des Beaux Arts Charleroi, Belgium, Casino Luxembourg.

**1996**

Exhibition held in Paris at the Galerie Nationale du Jeu de Paume, Paris with the assistance of the British Council. La Caixa de Pensiones, Barcelona; Museum of Modern Art, Dublin; Schirn Kunsthalle, Frankfurt am Main.

**1996-98**

First retrospective of works on paper curated by Michael Semff beginning at the Lenbachhaus Staatliche Graphische Sammlung, Munich and travelling throughout Europe, Milwaukee Art Museum, Denver Art Museum and the Brooklyn Museum, New York.

Sean Scully in his London Studio 1994
Photo: Catherine Lee

# Catalogue list

1. *River* 1984
   oil on canvas
   54 x 72"/ 137.2 x 182.9cm
   Private collection

2. *Stare* 1984
   oil on linen
   36 x 60"/ 91.4 x 152.4cm
   Private collection, London

3. *Tonio* 1984
   oil on canvas
   183 x 249cm
   Tate Gallery, presented by Janet
   Woolfson de Botton 1996

4. *Cross* 1986
   oil on canvas
   80 x 48"/203.2 x 122cm
   Private collection

5. *A Happy Land* 1987
   oil on canvas
   96 x 96"/ 243.8 x 243.8cm
   Tate Gallery, presented by Janet
   Woolfson de Botton 1996 to
   celebrate the Tate Gallery
   Centenary 1997

6.  *Battered Earth* 1988
    oil on canvas
    72 x 72"/ 182.8 x 182.8cm
    Private collection

7.  *White Window* 1988
    oil on linen
    96 x 146"/ 243.8 x 370.8cm
    Tate Gallery, purchased 1989

8.  *Without* 1988
    oil on canvas
    96 x 144"/243 .84 x 365cm
    Private collection

9.  *Red Painting* 1989
    oil on canvas
    36 x 48"/91.4 x 122cm
    Private collection

10. *Inisher* 1990
    oil on linen
    36 x 36"/ 91.4 x 91.4cm
    Private collection

11. *Skerry* 1992
    oil on canvas
    36 x 30"/ 91.4 x 76.2cm
    Private collection

12. *Eriskay* 1992
    oil on canvas
    91.5 x 76.2cm
    Private collection

13. *Rona* 1992
    oil on canvas
    12 x12"/ 30.5 x 30.5cm
    Private collection

14. *Coll* 1993
    oil on linen and metal
    60 x 90.2cm
    Private collection

15. *Tabarca* 1994
    oil on wood
    61 x 91.4cm/24 x 36"
    Private collection

16. *Skellig* 1995
    oil on wood
    12 x 12"/ 30.5 x 30.5cm
    Private collection

17. *Block* 1995
    oil on wood
    12 x 12"/ 30.5 x 30.5cm
    Private collection

18. *West of West* 1995
    oil on linen
    108 x 180" /274.3 x 457.2cm
    Sean Scully

19. *Passenger, White, White* 1997
    oil on canvas
    80 x 75"/ 203.2 x 190.5cm
    Mr and Mrs. Schüller-Voith, Munich